Be An Expert!™

Bugs

Erin Kelly

Children's Press®
An imprint of Scholastic Inc.

Contents

Know the Names

Be an expert! Get to know the names of these bugs.

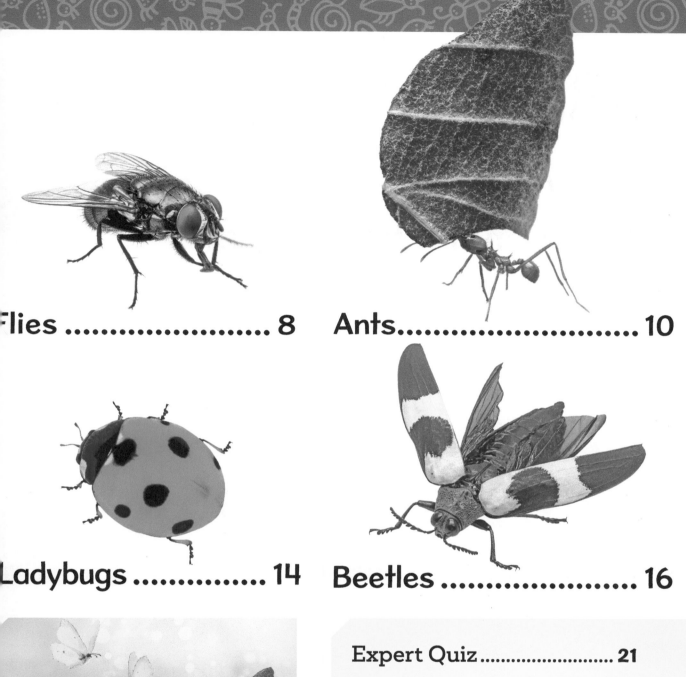

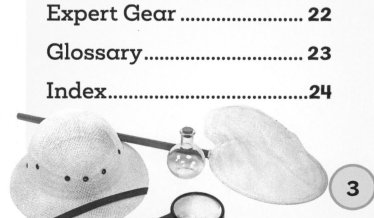

3

Bees

They buzz!
Some make honey too.

Zoom In

Find these parts in the big picture.

eyes   **wings**   **legs**   **stinger**

Butterflies

They help flowers grow!

caterpillar

Expert Fact

These insects are born as caterpillars. Then they become butterflies. This process is called **metamorphosis**.

Flies

They are hard to catch!

Brain Buzz

Q: How does a fly eat?

A: The fly vomits on the food, turning part of the food into liquid. Then the fly uses its **proboscis** to suck up the liquid.

proboscis

Ants

They build nests.
Some live underground!

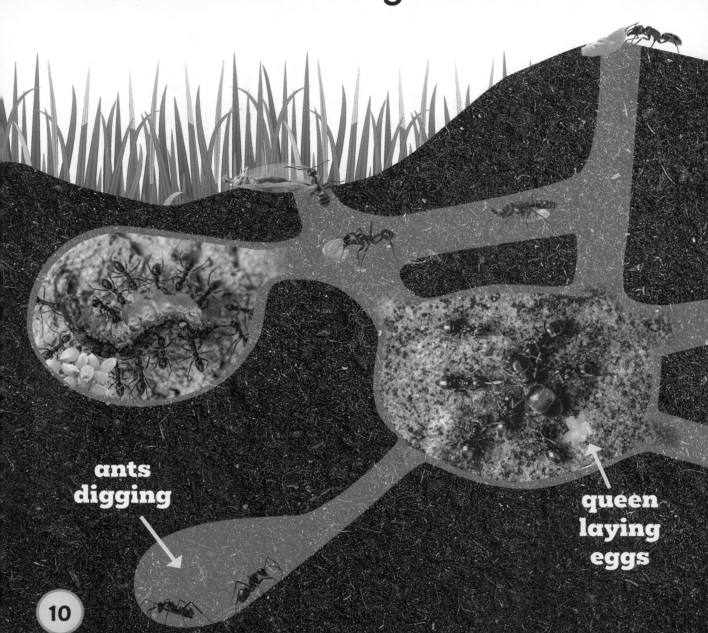

ants
digging

queen
laying
eggs

Expert Fact

Ants live and work together in a group called a colony. In the colony, ants do different jobs.

ants carrying food

ants storing food

ants caring for babies

Mosquitoes

They bite! Bites can be very itchy.

Brain Buzz

Q: Do all mosquitoes bite?

A: No. Only the females bite. They need to drink blood before they lay eggs.

Ladybugs

Most have spots!

Beetles

They come in many colors!

red-speckled
jewel beetle

shiny leaf
beetle

flower
longhorn beetle

jewel
beetle

stag beetle

red palm weevil

tansy beetle

Brain Buzz

Q: Can beetles be food?

A: Yes. Some people eat mealworms, which are the **larvae** of mealworm beetles. They are usually baked or fried!

Fireflies

Some light up!

Expert Fact

There are more than 20,000 **species** of fireflies. Different species have different flashing patterns.

All the Bugs

They are amazing.
Thank you, bugs!

1.

2.

5.

6.

Expert Quiz

Do you know the names of these bugs? Then you are an expert! See if someone else can name them too!

3.

4.

7.

8.

Answers: 1. Ladybug. 2. Mosquito. 3. Beetle. 4. Ant. 5. Butterfly. 6. Firefly. 7. Bee. 8. Fly.

21

Expert Gear

Meet a bug scientist, called an entomologist. What does she need to study bugs?

She has a **net**.

She has a **jar**.

She has a **camera**.

She has a **magnifying glass**.

Glossary

larvae (LAHR-vee): insects at the stage of development between egg and pupa, when they look like worms.

metamorphosis (met-uh-MOR-fuh-sis): a series of changes some animals go through as they become adults.

proboscis (pruh-BAH-sis): a long, tube-shaped mouth that some insects have.

species (SPEE-sheez): one of the groups into which animals and plants are divided.

Index

Library of Congress Cataloging-in-Publication Data
Names: Kelly, Erin Suzanne, 1965- author.
Title: Bugs/Erin Kelly.
Other titles: Be an expert! (Scholastic Inc.)
Description: New York: Children's Press, an imprint of Scholastic Inc., 2021. | Series: Be an expert! | Includes index. | Audience: Ages 4-5. | Audience: Grades K-1. | Summary: "Book introduces the reader to bugs"—Provided by publisher.
Identifiers: LCCN 2020006220 | ISBN 9781546100546 (library binding) | ISBN 9781546100560 (paperback)
Subjects: LCSH: Insects—Juvenile literature.
Classification: LCC QL467.2 .K46 2021 | DDC 595.7—dc23
LC record available at https://lccn.loc.gov/2020006220

Printed in North Mankato, MN, USA 150

SCHOLASTIC, CHILDREN'S PRESS, BE AN EXPERT!™, and associated logos are trademarks and/or registered trademarks of Scholastic Inc.

1 2 3 4 5 6 7 8 9 10 R 30 29 28 27 26 25 24 23 22 21

Scholastic Inc., 557 Broadway, New York, NY 10012.

Art direction and design by THREE DOGS DESIGN LLC.

Photos ©: cover background: Evgeniya Tiplyashina/123RF; cover flowers: Isselee/Dreamstime; cover, back cover, 1 girl: princessdlaf/Getty Images; back cover firefly: John Abbott/NPL/Minden Pictures; 2 top left: arlindo71/Getty Images; 2 bottom left: princessdlaf/Getty Images; 2 bottom right: John Abbott/NPL/Minden Pictures; 3 top left: eyup zengin/Getty Images; 3 top right: GlobalP/Getty Images; 5 bee with pollen: arlindo71/Getty Images; 5 inset top: UroshPetrovic/Getty Images; 7 inset: Bhushan Patil/EyeEm/Getty Images; 8, 9 fly: eyup zengin/Getty Images; 9 inset top: baona/Getty Images; 10 queen laying eggs: Stephen Dalton/Minden Pictures; 10 eggs: Pascal Goetgheluck/ardea.com/age fotostock; 10 ant with orange food: Jelger Herder/Buiten-beeld/Minden Pictures; 10 ant with green food: Poravute/Getty Images; 11 top right: GlobalP/Getty Images; 11 top left: Wavebreakmedia/Getty Images; 11 bottom: Malcolm Schuyl/Minden Pictures; 11 center: Nigel Cattlin/Alamy Images; 12 inset top: Tatyana Vychegzhanina/Dreamstime; 12 bottom: USDA/Science Source; 14 inset top: Jupiterimages/Getty Images; 16 shiny leaf beetle: MYN/Javier Aznar/NaturePL/Science Source; 18, 19 firefly: John Abbott/NPL/Minden Pictures; 19 inset: Sam Edwards/Getty Images; 20 bottom right: John Abbott/NPL/Minden Pictures; 21 top: princessdlaf/Getty Images; 21 center right: GlobalP/Getty Images; 21 bottom left: arlindo71/Getty Images; 21 bottom right: eyup zengin/Getty Images; 22: Valeriy Kirsanov/Dreamstime; 23 top: Nigel Cattlin/Alamy Images.

All other photos © Shutterstock.

Front cover: Beetle, butterflies, bee, and ladybugs. **Back cover:** Firefly.

Be An Expert!™

Some help flowers grow.
Some light up.
Some can be eaten!
What do you know about bugs?
With this book, you can become an expert!

Feel like a pro with exciting photos, expert facts, and fun challenges. Can you name which bug is a bee and which is a firefly? Try it! Then see if you can pass the Expert Quiz!

Read all the titles in the Be An Expert!™ series:

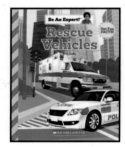

And many more!

Children's Press® an imprint of

www.scholastic.com/librarypublishing

ISBN: 978-1-5461-0056-0
90000

$5.99 US
$7.99 CAN

9 781546 100560

Be An Expert!™

Super Sharks

Erin Kelly

Get Fun FACTS!

SCHOLASTIC